Scientific review by the Clearwater Marine Aquarium
THE BEST SELLING STEM WITH ARTS BOOK SERIES
A REAL GIFT
BOOK 1
AGES 7+
GRADES 3 TO 5
CREATED BY
R. SUDAN MONTAGUEO
OCEAN BOWL SERIES
AF256179

Here's to #edutainment!

We work with other Non For Profits, Schools, After-school programs and their mission to support Literacy, S.T.E.A.M. , and Conservation.

Series: Ocean Bowl
Title: A Real Gift
Author: Roman Sudan Montagueo
Illustrator: Uzuri Designs
On-Sale Date: October 23rd, 2018
Publication Month: April 2021
Second Edition

Format: Paperback
ISBN: 978-0-9989794-6-5
E Book ISBN: 978-0-9989794-7-2
Library of Congress: 2018911179
Retail Price: $12.99 U.S.

Ages: 7 and Up
Grades: 3 and Up
Length: 157 Pages
Trim: 5.25 in. x 8 in.

Classification: Juvenile Educational (NF), Animals (F), Information Text (NF), Science & Nature (F), STEM, STEAM,

Important Note: If you see any mistakes or just want to provide feedback, send us an email. The third revision will be published 6 months from "on sale" date.

Creative Mindset Productions, LLC
1300 I St NW
Suite 400
Washington, D.C. 20005

For information, contact us at:
info@createmindset.com

If any material is quoted
all materials (story, illustrations, and characters) is protected material. Copyright © 2017

The Beautiful Game in the Sea!

OCEAN BOWL

"A REAL GIFT"

second edition

By R. Sudan Montagueo

Illustrated by Uzuri Designs

Creative Mindset Productions, LLC

Library of Congress Cataloguing-in-Publication Data available
ISBN: 978-0-9989794-6-5
E-Book ISBN: 978-0-9989794-7-2
Library of Congress: 2018911179

Made in the USA.
First printing 2018

FOREWORD

JASMINE ROSE, BSc - MARINE BIOLOGIST

This is a wonderful book which teaches children some great information about different animals that live in the ocean, and how they are all connected. We are so lucky to live on the planet that we do, and if we all share the passion and love for the ocean and its inhabitants that Jay does, then we will be able to enjoy and preserve our oceans for years to come. This book not only is extremely educational, it explains the dynamics between humans and animals in a way that is easy to understand, whilst highlighting how special that relationship is. The fact bubbles throughout the story allow children to see how the story is based on real events that occur, and the activities section allow the children to explore different ideas and helps them understand the information in a wonderful and engaging manner. I can't wait for future marine biologists to be inspired by this The Real Gift and the Ocean Bowl series. ----

CARLA BROOM, MRes - BIOLOGY and WILDLIFE CONSERVATIONIST

The Ocean Bowl series is not just a book about dolphins playing aquaball, it's a resource to teach kids about teamwork, friendship and our planet. Teaching about the ocean environment is vital to encourage people to respect and look after the natural world, and this book does just that, while keeping it entertaining and exciting! ----

(Short biographies are located at the end of this book.)

WHAT IS IN THIS BOOK?
(TABLE OF CONENTS)

ODON

He is named after the Norse chief god, who likes to wander and seek new adventures. He's Oria and Zac's fun caring dad and loves to play aquaball. He is the founder of the aquaball league where he's the G.O.A.T.... the M.J. of the game.

MARY ANNA

She's Odon's mate and mother of their children, Oria and Zac. She likes to be called Anna for short. Her name comes from a Hispaniola queen and means "golden flower". She's an oracalla dolphin. They are relatives of the killer (orca) whale. A true fan of the game, she is also an aquaball sports TV broadcaster.

ORIA

She is the free spirited daughter of Odon and Anna and Zac's twin. Another version of her name is Aura. Oriana means "wind, sunrise or golden haired". With a strong will power, don't doubt her capabilities. She's got skills. Girl Power!

ZAC

He is the talented, boisterous son of Odon and Anna. Zac's full name is Azacca, which means spirit guide of agriculture. He is a future star like his dad (he's like a young Kobe or Bron).

SQUIDDY

He is a colossal squid. He has just as many jobs as he has tentacles. He is the aquaball league official "one-squid" band, fish-cake chef, team uniform maker, and medic. Some squids can weigh up to 1000 pounds. They also have an ink sac. If threatened, they can shoot ink at their aggressors. They are often mistaken for the octopus.

PINKY

She is Oria's best friend. This fashionista has diva-like tendencies. Her favorite color is pink and she's also pink… so her nickname is Pinky (get it?). Did you know the average life span of a starfish is 35 years?

MAYDAY

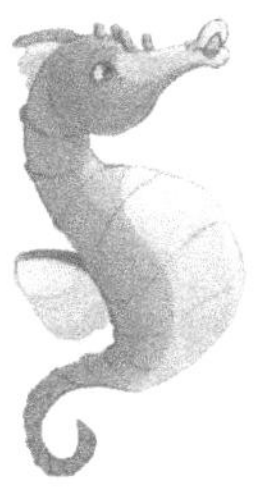

She's a real "smarty pants" for information. She's best friends with Oria and Pinky. Most seahorses have great eyesight, but she doesn't. Seahorses use their long snouts in tight spots to get food.

SOLITAIRE

He really likes to play aquaball. If you don't play by the rules and don't know the game structure; with a grudge, he will stare you down. He is a rough-toothed dolphin, which is a species of dolphin that is usually found in deep, warm-tropical waters around the world. Solitaire doesn't think humans are that smart either.

KRUG

He had a good and mild-mannered character before being corrupted by 8-Arms' sneaky manipulatios and greed. Krug is Odon's arch nemesis on the aquaball courts. He is a bottlenose dolphin.

MAGIX

This swift, athletically handsome common dolphin is one of the pinnacle super stars of the aquaball league. He has skills like the soccer superstar Christano Ronaldo.

TATER TOT CHIPS (A.K.A. TATER CHIPS)

He is an Atlantic humpback dolphin who is ALWAYS hungry. Don't let his shyness fool you. He's an awesome aquaball passer.

TOO SHORT TWO

He is a star aquaball half-back guard. His ego is big, but he has the speed and agility to get past his defenders. He is a spinner dolphin. They are famous for their acrobatic jumps and spins in tropical waters.

BON
A.K.A. BON BON

The smooth talking Bon is best friends with Odon, Solitaire and Rooks. They are a tight dolphin pod, and he is often the voice of wisdom,togetherness, and teamwork.

BOOTS

A good friend of Oria and Zac, Boots carries around an old pair of boots that he found in the sea. The dramatic episode of the laced boots caused him to choke. To conquer that fear, he wears and uses the boots.

8 ARMS

It's all business for this underwater boss. He owns a successful plankton fish chip business and is the team owner of the Argonauts aquaball club. Octopi have the natural ability to change colors to warn other animals that threaten them. If 8-Arms goes red, steer clear because that means he's very angry!

JAY

Jay is an energetic, adventurous boy who loves to do anything that involves being in the sea. He's an advocate of keeping the waters and land of JamRock Bay clean and safe. Jay can speak and understand multiple languages. He engineered a tool that helps him communicate with dolphins. He can also use sign language with dolphins.

PHOENIX

Phoenix is Jay's boat buddy. Most days, he doesn't feel like being bothered. This Bermudian long-tail bird journals the Aqua Ball games and occasionally "tries" to sing karaoke.

The following pages show the home of the pod squad. JamRock Bay is the sea port city that Jay lives and JamRock Bay Cove is where our favorite dolphins live.

JamRock Bay is a region of the Atlantis Prime Islands.

JAMROCK BAY
DOLPHINS COVE

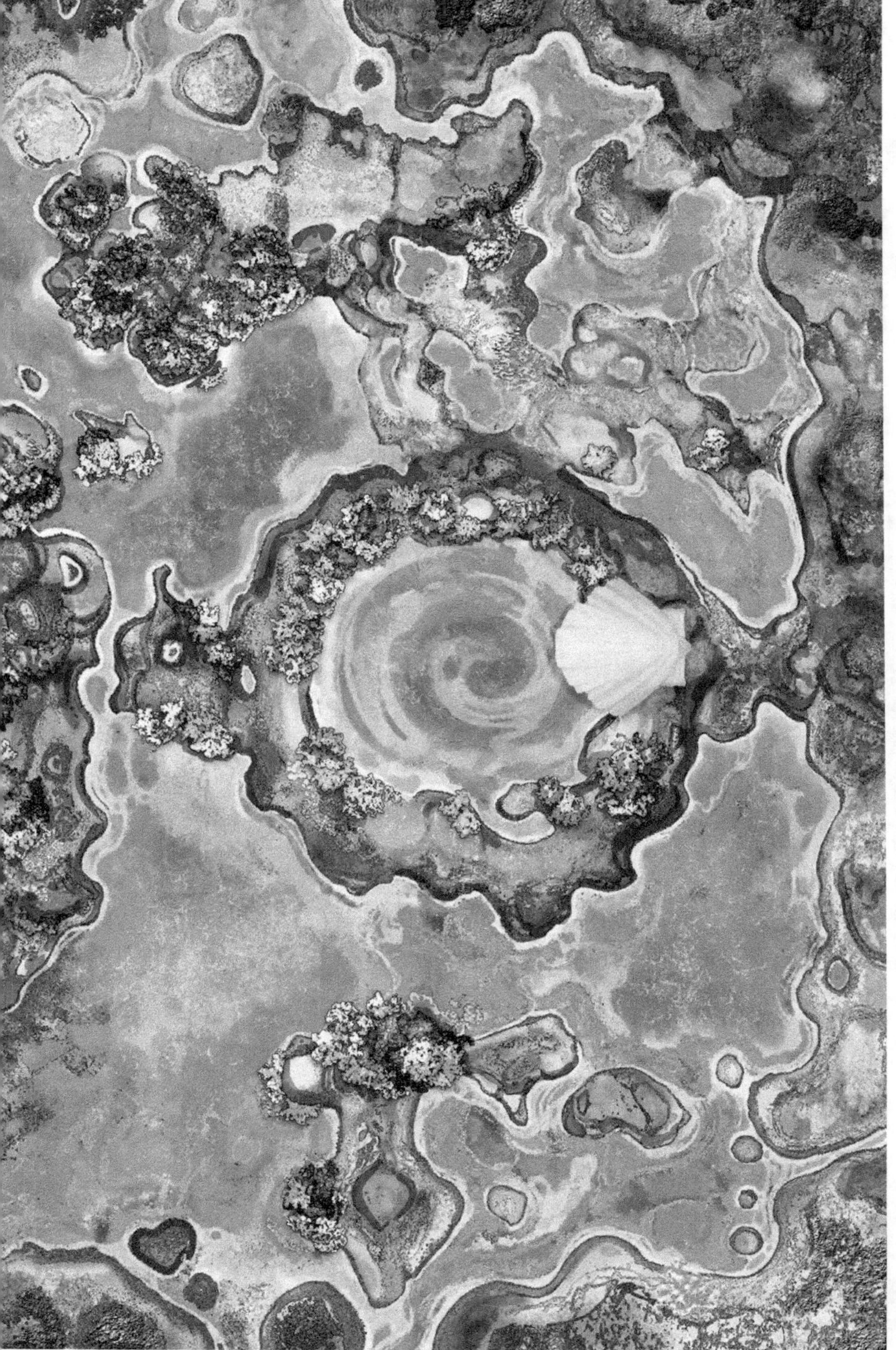

THE ISLES OF ATLANTIS PRIME

Neptunes Curse
The Crazy Dagger Sea
Genie Bayside
ating Rock Sea
Keys North
Ocean Bowl School 3
Valley of Leon de Marco
Sinbads Sound
The Buc Stops Here Cave
Carnival
Pirates Cove
Lira's Isle
Aqualand
St. Davees Reef
Quartz Island
Fortune Mountains
Black Mamba Peninsula
Kushu Land
Stingray Beach
Davvy Jones Pocket
Fort of Atlantis
Jordans Rock
Poseidon's Horn
Amazonian Shelter
ts of Oceana
Rocky Ridge
Isle of Monte Bleu
ean Bowl School 2
Oceana Bay

A GLIMPSE OF THE FUTURE GOAL

With one end of the roped ball in his mouth, Odon jets like a heat-seeking torpedo towards his opponents' giant clam goal. The clam goal has a friendly-looking toucan bird resting on top of it, keeping track of when the goals are scored. Odon feels comfortable at this moment, adrenaline pumping and fans cheering. This is the aquaball, and while it may not have been around for the longest time, he's already become one of the best there is.

The crowd is packed with many sea beings like dolphins, stingrays, turtles and many others. They all gather to catch a glimpse of the best rivalry in aquaball history. Odon and his team; the Tridents, jet-stream through the turquoise waters, past the cheerleading dolphins and the camera crew with Anna looking on.

"Here it comes!" Anna says excitedly. She nudges Scooter; the green sea turtle, with her nose. "Get your camera ready because you won't want to miss this." Scooter grabs the camera, takes it off his shelled back, and fixes it on Odon.

"Let's go, Odon!" yells Jay from his boat. He jumps up and down, making rippling waves with his rocking boat. "Show them why you're the best!"

Odon pushes the aquaball a little in front of him with his nose. He winds up and curls in a ball shape. He is preparing his special power move - the Speed Blast!

Lightning sparks and a glow flows around Odon as he unleashes the Speed Blast. He's moving so fast with the ball that he gets past the dolphin defending the clam and shoots the ball into the giant clam goal with a head bunt.

"Goaaaaaaaaaaal!" Shouts the toucan bird as he blows on his horn. The crowd goes wild for the athletically gifted right whale dolphin; Odon. He jumps into the air and sends a celebratory victory wave in Jay's direction. Seeing his friend cheering him on, Odon remembers that fateful day a storm rolled in and changed the course of his life for the better forever.

CHAPTER ONE

"A REAL GIFT"

Odon, the right whale dolphin, peeks his head over the mighty waves. His sleek, black-and-white body rockets through the ocean waters like a bullet. Splish-splash and dash! About twenty meters off the shoreline, he spies the silhouette of a boat and the profile of a familiar, kind face. It's Jay, the fishing kid.

"You know my family taught me how to boat and fish?" says Jay into a small device in his hand. "And you still can't understand me, yet can you?" Jay asks with a laugh. When Odon just stares and smiles, Jay realizes he was right. Shaking his head with a smile, he repeats his question in sign language.

The northern right whale and the southern right whale are two different species of whale? While they're not the same, they do have one thing in common: both of them are missing their dorsal fin! Instead, they have sloping foreheads, slimmer tails, and smaller flukes that make them more streamlined. These evolved, organic body parts allow them to make longer leaps and bounce over the ocean's surface.

"Northern Right Whale Dolphin," January 24, 2020.

https://us.whales.org/whales-dolphins/species-guide/ northern-right-whale-dolphin/.

"Southern Right Whale Dolphin," January 24, 2020.

https://us.whales.org/whales-dolphins/species-guide/ southern-right-whale-dolphin/

Normally, Jay and his dolphin friend communicate with each other using sign language, but Jay is also working on a genius idea: a vocal dolphin translator. He's working on it and plans to install it in his new gadget technology cannon. Jay is installing a grappling hook, a sonic gun, and also plans to install an equivalent option to convert the cannon into a water jet pack.

Jay learned everything he knows about fishing, the sea, and building things from his mentor and friend. His mentor and friend is Jay's only uncle, Tio. The ocean is Jay's love and life. It brings him great joy to feel the ocean breeze, fish, and occasionally dive in for a quick swim. Not to mention playing with his best friend in the sea, Odon.

Odon whistles to get Jay's attention.

"Hey buddy, you ready to go fishing?" Jay asks with a smile.

Echolocation is when dolphins produce high-frequency clicks in their nasal passage that passes through the melon, the fatty, rounded region of their forehead, which directs the sounds outwards. These sounds bounce off an object or creature in the ocean and echo back through the fatty cavity in the dolphin's jawbone. These evolved, organic body parts allow dolphins to navigate, communicate, or detect objects on or under the water's surface. Dolphins aren't the only animals to use echolocation, either. Owing to their poor eyesight and aided by their large ears, bats also use echolocation to navigate and find food.

"How Do Dolphins Communicate?" October 21, 2020.

https://us.whales.org/whales-dolphins/how-do-dolphins-communicate/

JAY

25

Odon bounces his head happily and darts under the water. He then uses his echolocation, a special ability that allows him to locate precisely where the fish are. Click! Click. Click! Odon releases his echolocation sound and immediately locates a school of pollock fish.

Odon swims around the entire school like a whirlwind tornado. Simultaneously, Jay casts his fishing pole and throws his net into the water, careful to keep it far away from Odon because swimming so fast and furiously, he could easily get tangled up, too. As Jay watches the waters churn from the fish, he struggles to catch any. At first, he feels frustrated. Then he remembers what his Tio always said: "You got this. Be patient. Be smart. Believe in yourself. Build your confidence, and then GO hard! You have 99 problems, but this isn't one of them."

"Build your confidence, you got this," he says to himself, "and then Go hard!" Jay pumps his fist in the air in excitement. "In other words," he continues, "whatever you do, work hard and do your best." Jay yells out, feeling reassured, "I got this!"

Whoosh! Whoosh! Whoosh! Around and around, Odon goes, circling the fish until they are clumped together like a knitted ball. Then he plunges through for a quick snack.

"Way to go, Odon!" Jay says as he pulls in a net full of large fish. "Dios mío! You sure are a better fisherman than I am," Jay says, slapping his leg and laughing heartily.

Dolphins can get tangled up in fishing nets. When they get tangled, these nets can actually drown them because it stops them from being able to rise to the surface to breathe! While some newer nets are designed to release dolphins, who are accidentally caught in them, over 650,000 marine mammals, including dolphins, whales, sea lions, and seals, still drown each year.

"Saving Our Seas from Harmful Fisheries." Fisheries. Accessed February 11, 2021.

http://www.biologicaldiversity.org/campaigns/fisheries/index.html

Jay had so much fun fishing with Odon. The two talked the afternoon away. At the end of the day, Odon and Jay agree that they need to go fishing tomorrow, too!

The next morning, Odon awakens to the

sound of sea lions noisily barking and splashing in the water. By mid-morning, Odon makes his way to where Jay would be fishing. He imagines all the pollock and herring they will catch together, but as Odon travels through the water, the winds start to pick up speed. Suddenly, the skies are painted grey, and a streak of silvery lightning flashes. Odon can feel it; a storm is coming.

Did You Know? No.4

Dolphins must stay awake to breathe! So, if they can't breathe when they are asleep, when do they sleep? Dolphins sleep by only using one half of their brain at a time. Isn't that wild!

"How Do Dolphins Sleep?" Whale & Dolphin Conservation USA, April 16, 2020.

https://us.whales.org/whales-dolphins/how-do-dolphins-sleep/

Odon knows he must warn his friend. He swims closer to Jay's boat and zigzags anxiously. When Jay spots Odon, he immediately knows something is wrong because he has never seen Odon behave like this.

"What's wrong?" But before Jay can finish his question, the winds pick up even faster. A big wave smashes into the broad side of the boat, flips it over, and tosses Jay into the turbulent sea. He tries to keep his head above the water, but the waves crash over him again and again.

Jays pleads, "Be easy on me, great sea." Instead of panicking, Jay remembers what Tio would say and uses it to encourage himself. "I got this!"

Odon dives to dodge the downpour of rain so he can find Jay. When he resurfaces, he searches frantically, but Jay and his boat are nowhere to be seen. Lightning crackles over the waves and finally spots Jay's head bobbing before his friend sinks under again. He bolts across the distance, swimming faster than he's ever done before. This is one of the strongest storms Odon has ever experienced, but he can't afford to let Jay down.

Did You Know? **No.5**
Dolphins can sense changes and dangers in their environment, like an oncoming tropical storm or a hurricane. Scientists think this response might be because they detect a saltwater difference after a large number of freshwater rainfalls. With their strong survival instinct and intelligence, they can take precautions to stay safe, dive deep, or swim out into deeper waters.

Dunn, Jon. "What Do Dolphins Do during Storms?" August 19, 2020.

Finally, he discovers Jay, and with his friend hanging on tightly to the capsized boat, he drags him up to the surface. Jay coughs out water and hugs Odon tightly.

"Yeah, you got me. Thanks, old friend," Jay sputters and pats Odon. Tuckered out, Jay rests his cheek against the Odon's striped neck as he carries him towards the shore to safety. After such a big scare, Jay isn't sure what he should do. Each morning, Jay walks out to his boat and looks out to the open waters. Is it worth chancing a sea storm again to be on the water? What do you think, Tio? Jay thinks to himself. Should I keep being on the ocean? Or should I stick to shore and leave my flippered friend behind?

Days pass, and Odon still hasn't seen Jay at his normal fishing spot. Even though he hadn't seen his friend, Odon still swims to Jay's usual fishing spot. In his heart, he knows his friend will come again. Sure enough, as Odon gets closer, he notices a weathered fishing boat with a familiar shape on deck.

Then, he recognizes Jay's lilting voice singing along with his favorite tune on the ship's radio. Odon whistles loudly and spirals high up into the air while Jay watches in amazement.

"I'm happy to see you too, my friend!" Jay shouts as Odon approaches the boat. He rubs the side of Odon's nose and slaps him a high fin. "I have a special treat for you today." He pulls out a ball with a rope rung through on each side of its sphere from his bag. Odon looks at it strangely. "I know I haven't been around lately, but I came up with this awesome idea!" He motions for Odon to come closer. "Now watch me, amigo!" Jay throws the ball in the air, catches it between his knees, and then juggles it by kicking his feet in an alternating pattern. Left foot, right foot, knee; right foot, left foot--Odon's head follows the ball as Jay passes it from knee to knee and then bounces it up to his head.

"One, two, three," Jay counts, punting the ball with his head before allowing it to fall back

down onto his knees. He dribbles the ball down the boat's side and then hits it into a big net onboard.

"Scoooreeeee… And the crowd goes wild!" Jay pumps his fists in the air as he shakes and shimmies in a happy dance.

Odon smiles and laughs. At first, Odon was nervous Jay had decided not to come back, but now that he sees the amazing new game, Odon does a backflip in excitement.

"Looks fun, right? Okay, your turn," Jay speaks and hand signs, then he tosses the ball into the water.

Odon rushes for the ball and flaps his tail to propel it into the air. He positions his head, ready for its landing.

BOOP! It plops onto the dolphin's head and rests there. Odon flips the ball high in the air, then somersaults backward and pounds the ball towards the net on deck.

"Say what!?!" says Jay in shock and awe. "Like a true pro," he applauds Odon.

Odon shows off by spy-hopping vertically on his tail across the surface and squeals at Jay. He thinks to himself, What a fun game! I've gotta show this off. Odon and Jay spend the rest of the day playing together. When the day comes to an end, Odon tries to return the ball before Jay leaves.

"Keep it. It's my gift to you," Jay says to Odon. "Though I can never repay you for saving my life."

Odon nods his head excitedly in thanks.

"I'm sure you and some other friends of yours will have a ball. Get it? Ball!" Jay says with delight and slaps his leg again. Odon waves one fin to signal his departure and makes plans to show his friends the exciting new game.

"I'm sure you and some other friends of yours will have a ball. Get it? Ball!" Jay says with delight and slaps his leg again. Odon waves one fin to signal his departure and makes plans to show his friends the exciting new game.

Did You Know? No.6

There are many stories of dolphins saving people and other animals, including other dolphins! It is common for dolphins to help the sickly pod mates by swimming alongside them to reach the surface and breathe in the wild. While there are many different ideas of why dolphins help people, one theory is that dolphins can use their echolocation to hear a human's heartbeat and then sense that the person is in danger.

Dolphins-World. "Dolphins Rescuing Humans."
Accessed February 10, 2021.

https://www.dolphins-world.com/dolphins-rescuing-humans/

CHAPTER TWO

"A NEW GAME KICKS UP"

After saying goodbye to Jay, Odon dashes off with his gift in tow. He can't wait to show his friends the super-cool tricks he can do with his new ball. Soon, he spots some of his friends' dolphins playing and exploring the local area. As soon as they see him, Odon's friends tilt their heads curiously at him. Odon has the ball by one rope end, wrestling it back and forth, waving it excitedly at them as they swim his way curiously. "Bon! Come check out this awesome new thing Jay gave me!" Odon says. Bon swims up to him faster, eager to check things out. When he gets there, he bumps Odon's gift with his nose.

"What is this?" He asks as he tilts his head from side to side. "This," Odon says proudly with a toss of his head, "is my new ball!" Odon tosses it high in the air and then uses his neck to catch it.

"Woah, totally cool!" Two new dolphins Odon has never met before swim up to join them. The smaller of the two dolphins winks one of his squinty eyes at Odon.

"Doesn't look, too hard," he says,

"Yeah, right," Bon says. He flicks his tail playfully at the new dolphin. "You gotta ignore him, Odon. This is Solitaire, and he thinks he's the best at everything." Bon motions to the other dolphin. "And this is Rooks."

"Sup," Rooks and Solitaire both say at the same time.

ACTIVITY TIME-OUT...
IM SCOOTER. LETS DO THE ACTIVITY ON PAGE 157.

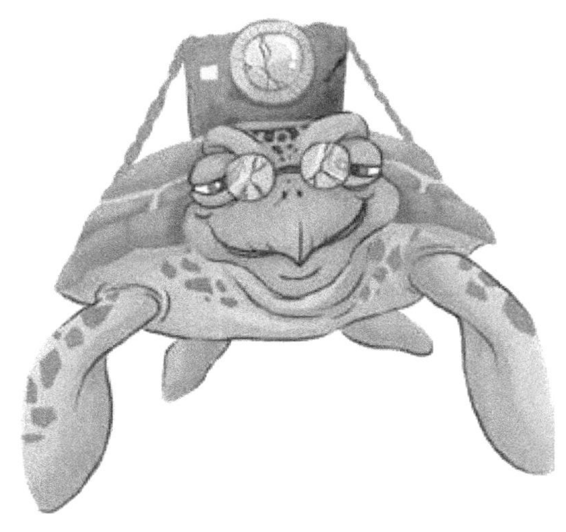

Odon flips the ball again and catches it with his tail this time. "Well, Solitaire, I hate to burst your bubble, but I think I've already got you beat for the best with this."

"Ayyy Ohh!" They all laugh when Solitaire blows bubbles in Odon's face.

"Toss it here, and let's see who's the best."

"Not before I get a chance to try my tail at it," says Bon. Odon laughs and tosses him the ball. Bon flips it up and then blows a stream of air from his blowhole at the ball to make it spin. Then he passes the ball to Rooks, who gives Solitaire the ball, pushing it back over to Odon. The new pals keep at this awhile, increasing the tempo and widening their playing circle.

"Hey, hey, look at this," Bon says as he rockets the ball high into the air. He flies up after it and spikes it from mid-air.

"Wiickkeeedddd!" Solitaire expresses.

"That's impressive," Odon says. Rooks nods his head in agreement.

"Nice!" He says. "Let's take this party to a place with more space," Rooks suggests.

"I think I know the perfect spot!" Bon says, and then he leads them to a nearby lagoon. When they get there, Odon says, "Let me show you guys something. Keep your eyes on the open giant clam over there." Odon gets the ball, aims, and hits it with his fin. It shoots straight into the clam. "I got that!"

"Goal! Awesome shot!" Bon says.

The gang shouts, "Nice!"

As the day wears on, Odon, Bon, Rooks, and Solitaire continue playing. Soon, it feels like

Odon has known the three other dolphins for a long time, even though it's only Bon that he's met before that day. They aren't like the dolphins Odon normally hangs out with, but Odon has always enjoyed meeting new sea-folk.

"So," Odon says as they all stop to catch their breath, "are you guys from the Rock like Bon?"

"The same!" says Solitaire. "We are all from the Rock—JamRock Bay. In fact, why don't we hightail it over to the Trini's Lagoon Courts at JamRock Bay? You'll love the courts there if you like playing here," says Solitaire as he retrieves the ball. Nervously, Odon agrees. He's heard that JamRock Bay was one of the coolest places in the whole ocean, and now he was getting a chance to visit.

When they get there, Odon does his best to act like he's not shocked by the sheer number of dolphins there. They're everywhere!

It is like a super-duper pod. The Courts in the lagoon have the remains of a tall sailing ship that sank near the cliffs in a narrow passage of water between the mainland and an island called a sound. The shipwreck at the Courts was submerged for years until the sea creatures in the JamRock Bay decided it would make a great place to hang out and play. They decorated its masts and galleys with colorful corals, seaweeds, and shells. Above the water, seagulls are busy working as waiters serving snacks, and everyone is jamming to the beats of the hit hip-hop group of white-beaked dolphins, known as The Boogie Boys. The three lead performers stand at the

In the great blue ocean, many types of dolphins hang in groups called "pods." They can range in size from anywhere from 2-30 members. However, they can also form "superpods" in deeper parts of the ocean containing thousands of dolphins. Another type of dolphin pod is a juvenile pod. Juvenile pods include both males and females, but males often stay in these pods longer. Dolphins use whistles to communicate with each other. Every dolphin has a unique whistle pattern, called a "signature whistle."

"Dolphin Facts and Information." Whale & Dolphin Conservation USA, November 30, 2020.

https://us.whales.org/whales-dolphins/facts-about-dolphins/#:~:text=The%20smallest%20dolphins&text=A%20group%20of%20dolphins%20is,for%20food%20as%20a%20team

front of the stage, coral mics in hand, singing and rapping while moving in intricate patterns. Behind them, back up dancers are gliding in and out, balancing clam beatboxes on their shoulders while a Beluga whale spins on its head in the middle. One by one, it feels like every eye turns to stare at Odon with the tail end of the rope attached to the ball in his mouth.

Reluctant at first, Odon finally decides to start up a game between the guys when he sees two giant clams. "Yo! See those bad boys? We can use them as goals. One on this end of the field, and let's put the other goal on the other end."

"Can we move those claims without permission?" Asks Rooks. "I don't know if the owners would appreciate that very much."

"True," says Odon, feeling sad that his idea might fall through.

"I know!" Bon says. "Solitaire, can you go ask the giant clam owners? They can be the scorekeepers and referees."

"Great idea!" Solitaire water-sprints over to the clam owners. The music slowly fades away as everyone looks to see what Odon and his newfound pod crew are doing. Odon blushes a little as he notices a beautiful young dolphin smiling at him.

Solitaire returns with a big smile on his face. "The clam owners are so in, dudes! This is going to be awesome." Odon doesn't hear him. Instead, he waves at the girl, who is still smiling widely at him.

"You, dude!" Bon says, bumping him to get his attention. "We need some rules, right?"

"Who needs rules?" Solitaire says. "They just get in the way," he says good-naturedly.

"Yea, get in the way of you cheating." Bon laughs.

"I don't cheat. I'm a winner, baby!"

Odon laughs at Solitaire. "I agree with Bon. Let's make some rules. If I shoot and score the ball into the giant clam goal from zero to three meters out, then I score one point. If I shoot and score from four meters or further, then it's worth two points," says Odon.

"Great! But what can we use?" someone from the pod of dolphins pitches in. "Our fins, our tails?"

"Anything dolphin," Odon replies with a smile and demonstrates. "A spin," as he dashes from the water and does a complete 360-degree turn in the air. When he lands back in the water with the ball, he shouts out, "A fin," and then smacks the ball towards Bon with his fin to pass it. Bon passes Solitaire the ball. Solitaire juggles the ball on his nose. "And, of course," laughs Odon, "A nose." Solitaire shoots the ball into the giant clam goal. Odon cheers! "Head, echolocation, anything a dolphin can do, it goes. Each team, which consists of four players on the field of play, will have three downs before the other tries to stop them by tackling or stealing the ball. The team with the most points wins!"

Did You Know? No. 8
Dolphins love to play! In fact, playing is not all fun and games for them. When dolphins play, they are also learning about social cues, creating strong bonds, and entertaining their highly intelligent minds. Dolphin's sleek bodies can perform acrobatic leaps and spins above the surface of the water, and they can even be observed in something that looks like play fighting with each other and forming strong bonds. We often see wild dolphins playing with a field of seagrass and other objects in their environment like snail egg casings. However, even though dolphins are playful and friendly by nature, like wild animals, it is important not to force ourselves into their space and observe them from afar.

It is best to let dolphins be dolphins! We can view them in the wild safely, free of human interaction.

Kuczaj, S. A., & Eskelinen, H. C. (2014). Why do dolphins play? Animal Behavior and Cognition, 1(2), 113-127. doi: 10.12966/abc.05.03.2014

"Sounds like my kind of rush! We have our pod squad. Me, Bon, Rooks, and Solitaire," he points out his players to the fellas.

"Who wants to play?" Odon asks the crowd in the lagoon. Without hesitation, many fins go up.

"Man, that's a whole lot!" Bon says. "Who would have thought the game would be this hot already?"

"I think you mean who would have thought we'd have so many fans already," Rooks says with a giggle as he notices the girls.

"You mean MY fans," Solitaire says.

"Oh no," Bon says. "They're going to be cheering me on." He winks at the girls, and they all roll their eyes. "What? No love for me!" He calls after them jokingly. "Not even from you, Anna?" Odon's heart races as he sees the girl who had been smiling at him start to swim over.

"H-h-hi," Odon stammers out when Anna arrives. "My name is Odon."

"Hi there," Anna says.

"What about me?" Bon says.

"What about you?" says Anna without taking her eyes off Odon. Rooks and Solitaire laugh and nudge Bon playfully.

"Ouch, Mary Anna!"

Anna rolls her eyes and smiles at Bon. "You're lucky we're already friends, Bon," she chuckles. "Nobody ever calls me anything other than Anna, and you should know that best. Or don't you remember what happened last time you called me something other than my name?"

"Ohhhh, she bites!"

"That's what teeth are for," Anna laughs. "Or did the time you cracked yours trying to eat rock make you forget?" Everyone dies laughing at Anna's joke.

"I like a girl who can stand up for herself."

"Smooottthhh," Solitaire says.

"I think it is," Anna says.

Unsure what to say next, Odon blurts out, "could you keep the clock?"

"Sure thing!" Anna swims back to give the guys space to play.

With one last look at Anna, Odon goes to where his team is already huddled up.

"So, where were we guys? Who's down to play my pod squad?" Odon asks. He scans the crowd of dolphins with their fins up and picks one from the crowd to captain the opposing team. The dolphin picks three other teammates to join him and then folds his fin arms to signal he's ready to throw down.

"Wait!" Solitaire says as he sees a blue tang fish speeding by. He grabs it by the tail and then tosses it up, up, up! "Call it," he says. "Heads or tails?"

"Tails!" says the dolphin captain.

The blue tang yells, "Weeeeeeee", in excitement as it rotates and comes splashing head first back into the water. It shakes its head to clear its vision. "What a ride!" He says to Solitaire. "Thanks for the thrill, man!"

"Anytime," Solitaire says with a laugh. Then he turns to the other captain and says, "Heads. Our ball!"

One dolphin squeal, "Two crab cakes. Three crocodiles' tails. Let's shake and bake!" The game begins, and Odon passes the ball to Bon, who immediately shoots it into the Argonaut's giant clam for one point. The spectators click and whistle with glee. The other team dashed forward and fast breaks the ball to score also. They add their own style of jumps, spins, and flips.

Odon and the other dolphins have so much fun that they don't stop playing until the clam owners remind them how long they've been playing.

"Coming down to snooze time, boys," one of the owners of the giant clams announces. At the end of the last goal, many of the dolphins approach Odon before leaving the Courts and ask him to come again with his ball. Odon is about to part ways with his boys when Bon asks him, "What do you call this game?"

"Yeah, Odon. You must have a name for this game!" Solitaire says. Rooks nods his head vigorously and grins.

"Well, I guess I'll call it aquaball!" decides Odon.

"Yeah, that's the perfect name!" Bon says. All the other dolphins nod in agreement.

Under the moonlit night, Odon and Anna catch each other's eyes again. Odon swims circles around her.

"So, you think you're all that now, huh?" says Anna with a wink and a headbutt.

"I will be someday. Just watch, Anna. I'm going to be something unstoppable," Odon replies.

"Yea," she agrees. "You know, I believe you will be."

"You know, I have a good feeling about you. Can you feel that we click? Get it? Click?"

"You're too much," smiles Anna.

They swim off together past the blue lights of the Lantern fish and the Bamboo coral. Odon says with one eyebrow raised and slightly turned head, "You know this could be the start of something cool."

CHAPTER THREE

"OCEAN BOWL 1 -- AQUABALL CHAMPIONSHIPS"

Three years after that first game, Odon is excited to see how quickly aquaball was catching on in the ocean community. Before he knew it, multiple teams were forming, and competitions were being held. Odon, Rooks, Bon, and Solitaire continue practicing aquaball, and with Anna promoting their awesome skills by featuring them in the JamRock Bay Ocean Net Boards and even a few highlight interviews that got tons of 'chirps' on social media, they soon make a name for themselves for being the best.

Within a year, an aquaball sports league was created to play the beautiful game in the sea. Jay was thrilled that his heartfelt gift to Odon was turning into something that was changing his friend's life and bringing together sea beings from all corners of the ocean.

But it wasn't their increasing popularity or Odon's amazing ability to dominate the court that was the most exciting part of aquaballs development. It was the league championship that was the most spectacular experience: Ocean Bowl. It would provide the dolphins with a great opportunity to play and show off their skills.

The first aquaball playoffs were exciting. Dolphins were dunking the aquaball, and they were shooting twos from almost half-court. There were fish cakes and chip snacks everywhere, and 'fin-tastic' bands tailgating parties. From his boat, Jay dances as he works on his gadget technology cannon (GTC) designs. With a screwdriver in his hand and a bucket cap on his head, Jay moonwalks across his boat.

"Go, Jay! Go, Jay! Go! Go!" Odon and Anna cheer. Jay turns his cap backward and pops and locks, making Odon and Anna cheer louder. Suddenly Phoenix, the Bermudian long-tail bird, warns Odon of some incoming plastic waste building up on the side of the boat and in the sound.

"If we don't clean the water, we'll have to cancel the Ocean Bowl. There's no way we can play with all that trash. It's not safe for any of us."

"What can we do?" Asks Anna, ready to help in any way she can.

"I don't know," Odon admits with a frown. "Trash and debris can hurt us. I hate to admit this, but we may have to cancel the game." Odon turns away, and Anna swims to his side and comforts him.

"I can't just stand around and let that happen!" Jay announces. He turns in the direction of the trash build-up. "I vow to help clean this mess up," says Jay, "but I'll need your help, amigo."

"Anything!" Odon says.

"I'll need you to herd the trash towards my boat, and then I'll use my new GTC to throw a net out and clean everything."

"Is that thing going to work this time?" Anna asks. "I've seen you working on it, and it's been pretty buggy."

Jay gives a huge thumbs up. "Trust me! I've got this." Odon quickly swims and lumps the trash together near Jay's boat. Jay then gets an idea to use the fishing net from his GTC to capture the trash. He throws the net over the side and begins to drag all the trash into the nets.

They smile, cheer, and shout out, "Way to go!" as Jay finishes loading the rest of the plastic waste on the boat. Jay and Odon turn their attention back to the games. Jay turns to Odon and yells, "Let the game begin!" Odon does a backflip and races off to join his team. Odon and his team, the athletic and smooth Tridents, are going up against the intimidating, strong, and skillful Argonauts led by a bottlenose dolphin named Krug.

Gracefully dancing on waves like jet ski boats, the dolphins use their dynamic abilities to swim, jump, and tumble in and out of the water as they warm up with the ball. The referee whistles for the first half of the game to start and outshoots Odon with the jump ball. The propelled power generated by Odon's fluke and flippers helps to rocket him to the giant clam's base and score the opening goal.

Krug looks at the scoreboards and grimaces. "My name will be up there soon," he promises. The rest of the Argonauts nod their head in agreement. They want to return the favor and score themselves. Their team strategist, Brigs, decides to dive deep into the mud to murk up the waters and hide the return offense. The Tridents are thrown into confusion because they can't see the ball or the opposing dolphins.

OCEAN BOWL 1

Tridents vs. Argonants

KRUG

"Whooshing like a tuna escaping a fisherman's net and out of a dark cloud of mud and water spins the new young star for the Argonauts– Krug!" Narrates the announcer.

Quick as a swordfish, Krug springs up from behind the Tridents and materializes behind their defines near the goal. "Hey boys," he whistles," over here!" With a satisfied grin, he taps the ball into the goal.

"Goaaaaaallllllll!!!!!" says the announcer. "Tridents and Argonauts tie at 1-1! What a game, folks, and we're just getting started!"

Odon clicks in frustration. Krug is good, he thinks to himself. But not better than me. I can do this! I've worked hard for this. It's time for all that practice to pay off. In a blink, Odon rushes off and rejoins the game with more determination.

The whale announcer reports: "Rook passes the ball to Bon then proceeds to block the entire defensive line. Solitaire does a quick swim step and back tails a pass over to Odon. Odon is swimming and pushing the ball through the waters like a missile with a heat signature towards the goal. Oh no! he gets blocked and cut off – he loses the ball. He does a quick high jump and spin to get control of the ball again by hitting the ball into the air!"

The crowd goes wild, and Anna spins in a tight circle. "Go, Odon!"

"It's a dolphin jump ball!" The game announcer comments as Odon and one of his opponents leap up after the ball but misses. "The Tridents have it back. Bon fakes the pass, shoots, and scores on the rookie, Krug! The score is now

2-1 for the Tridents!"

Krug gives Bon a mean, smug face to intimidate him. "That's the last bucket your team gets on me today," he says.

Odon swims up and smiles a little. He shrugs it off because he knows he can't let his opponent mess with teammates' heads. "Don't worry about what he says, Bon." Odon turns to Krug and frowns. "Drop the hate, man. Being competitive is great, but never make it too personal or take it that seriously. It's a game, you know. Remember we're supposed to have fun, and that means EVERYONE has fun," says Odon to Krug.

"Whatever, man," Krug says. "It's only halftime, and I'm not even close to being done yet."

"Thanks for sticking up for me, Odon," Bon says.

"Of course. That's what friends and teammates are for." Together, Bon and Odon swim with the rest of their team towards the locker room. The halftime score is 2-1 in favor of the Tridents. As the teams head to their respective watery locker rooms, the announcer begins to introduce the half-time entertainment.

Before he can make it into the locker room, Odon is scurried to the side to be interviewed by another league commentator. He holds a coral mic in one fin and a recorder in another. Leaning in close, the commentator says to Odon, "The league is taking off like wildfire."

"Well, it's all about the fans," Odon responds as he rotates to point his flippers as if introducing the crowd as the star of the show.

"Well, it has accumulated a lot of fans. One of them is your mate, Anna. How is it having your mate cheer you on as a league commentator?" Odon winks at her with affection in his eyes. She smirks back at him.

"She always seems to have the hardest questions for me to answer," he admits with a laugh. "In fact," he says as he notices her coral mic in her fin pressed against her beginning to bulge belly, "I think she has one of the questions for me now.

Anna turns serious, and with a business-like dolphin posture, she interviews her mate. "Odon, your Tridents are number one. The league has grown quickly. They have teams separated into four divisions with two teams each," says Anna as she describes the league and its growth. "The teams have home lagoons and aquaball courts around the world. The divisions are the Arctic, Caribbean, Pacific, and Atlantic. Your most popular teams to date are the Cyclones, the Tridents, the Harpoons, and your arch-rivals; The Argonauts. These are exciting times for you and the league. Your fans want to know what's coming next?" asks Anna. There is a pause from Odon as he soaks up the admiration from the crowds of sea lions, otters, stingrays, and dolphins from all over the world.

"Your biggest fans all want to know," Anna asks again. "Are you retiring soon to be the full-time owner of the Tridents and a new dad?" Anna pauses, and they both blush. This is a conversation they have had many times before. Odon knows what Anna hopes for after the Ocean Bowl. She wants him to step away from playing on the court and step into a manager position. But the truth is, Odon still isn't sure which one he wants. He loves aquaball with all his heart, and he isn't sure just being a manager will be enough for him. Unsure of what to say to Anna, he clears his throat and looks away shyly.

As if she can read his mind and see his uncertainty and Anna laughs off her questions. "I guess we'll all have to wait and see what the superb and legendary aquaball player, Odon, does next with his career. I, for one, know that whatever it is will be amazing." She smiles reassuringly at him. Then, before Odon can answer, Anna throws one more question his way. "Do you see any challenges to growing and capturing the championship?"

Odon sighs in relief. This is a question he can answer. "There is always a challenge lurking in the shadows," Odon says with confidence. "But whatever obstacles come, I got this!"

Just over his shoulder, Bon and the team shout, "WE GOT THIS."

Both the commentator and Anna smile at the team's comradery and spirit. "Thanks for the time Odon. You're kind of cool," Anna says with a wide grin. "Back to you guys in the booth," she says as she points her mic to the grandstand where the booth is.

"Thanks, guys," Odon beams and points to the crowd. The aquaball fans start clapping and splashing to cheer on their favorite star. Odon marvels at the fact that the fans are this excited even though his team is only up 2-1. He knows that the Argonauts will be working extra hard to make a comeback. Taking one last look at the board, Odon turns and approaches the field. Rooks swims over to him. "It's crazy, isn't it," he says.

"What do you mean?"

"This," Rooks gestures to the stands, who have various jerseys and signs with their team name on them. "Who would have thought that four friends would end up here all those years ago."

Odon chuckles. "Not me."

"Me either," Rooks admits. "Back then, I was always a little nervous about the future, you know. I didn't have a lot of dreams, and I didn't know where I was going in life. But the aquaball has given me a chance to change all that. It's given me a chance to be somebody, you know?"

"But Rooks, you were somebody before all this."

"Sure, but not like you, Odon. One look at you, and everyone knew you would be some fishy. One look at me and well," he shrugs, "one look at me, and people would look right through me. But this game," Rocks smiles, "this game gave me new life, man. I don't know where I'd be without it."

"Oh man, I didn't know you felt like that!"

"You know what's crazy," Rooks says as he looks out into the audience, "imagine all the calves who are watching us now. We get to have a hand in writing a playbook they may hope to see their future in. We get to give them someone they can

look up to. We get to be some-fishy to them."
Odon and Rooks gaze back over the audience again. Odon spots a mother in the stands who sits with her calf. The calf bounces excitedly in the waves and points towards Odon's team. This isn't just about me; Odon thinks to himself. This is about them. They're watching, and whoever wins will be the example of what it means to be a winner. Everywhere he looks, Odon can see excitement building as the stadium prepares for the second half of the first-ever Ocean Bowl! With one last look at the crowd, the fans, and the owner's boxes, Odon turns to get ready to play.

LET S TAKE A BREAK. FUN ACTIVITY TIME.

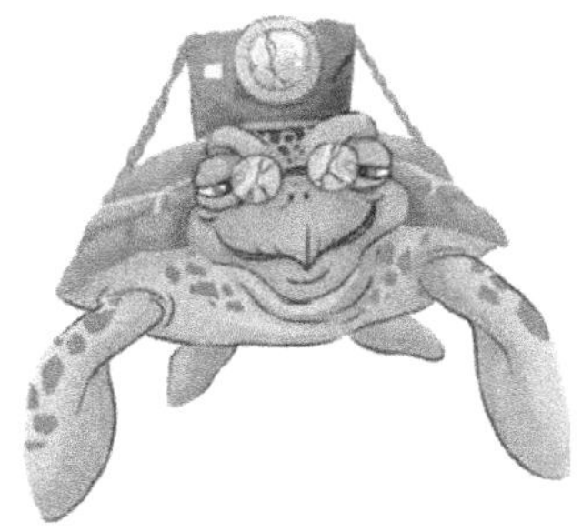

"Count them up" (Addition Math Problem)

**Write and solve an addition
equation for each problem.**

1. The city zoo has four Atlantic
Bottlenose Dolphins and five Pacific
white-side dolphins. How many
dolphins does it have in all?

$$4 + 5 =$$

2. The parrot house has six adu t
macaws and nine young macaws.
How many macaws does it have in
all?

_______ + _______ = _______

3. "They got what?" The Underground
Display has nine mother koalas. Three
of them each have one baby. How
many koalas are there in all?

_______ + _______ = _______

5. Two years ago, the anaconda snake
measured nine feet long. This year it
grew another nine feet. How many
feet long is it this year?

_______ + _______ = _______

5. The Polar Ice World has seven
penguins and four harp seals. How
many polar animals are there in all?

_______ + _______ = _______

6. Tater Chip eats eight baskets of
fishchips a day.
How many baskets of fish chips does
he eat in two days?

_______ + _______ = _______

CHAPTER FOUR

"99 PROBLEMS"

From the owner's box of the Argonauts, a dark brown octopus named 8-Arms with red highlights hangs inside a large treasure chest overflowing with sea coins and snacks.

accident, in time, it can grow back!

Newman, Alan. "Alan Newman," October 5, 2016.

http://www.scijourner.org/2016/05/20/the-magic-of-arm-regrowth/#:~:text=Octopi%20regenerate%20lost%20arms%20just,grow%20into%20a%20new%20octopus.&text=As%20soon%20as%20the%20arm,immediately%20begins%20its%20regeneration%20process.

"Octopuses Keep Surprising US - Here Are Eight Examples How." Accessed February 11, 2021.

https://www.nhm.ac.uk/discover/octopuses-keep-surprising-us-here-are-eight-examples-how.html#:~:text=Octopuses%20have%20about%20as%20many

He has a broken fedora hat sitting askew on his head and three overlapping rusted chains around his neck with his name stamped on a gold plate attached to one chain. The notorious underworld snack boss shovels seaweed snacks into his clacking beak. He cackles at a dolphin with eyeglasses that hovers meekly in front of him.

"You don't become the owner of every worthwhile route and company that supplies seaweed chips, fish chips, and fish patties without knowing how to do business." He says between crunches. "And this," 8-Arms thrusts one of his arms towards the aquaball field, "is how to do business!", as 8-Arms refers to the sales transaction between the large crowd buying snacks and marketing banners around the stadium.

"I'm begging you Mr. 8-Arms. Don't take my team the Argonauts from me. I fell behind in credit payments by six months. Is this how you do business? By forcing someone to hand over their aquaball team? My life... my love." Asks the dolphin with the glasses. He flinches when 8-Arms glares at him.

"It's not my fault you didn't pay your credit bill. You're lucky I'm feeling nice. You could be floating belly side up, you know." 8-Arms inspects one of the suckers on one of his tentacles. "It's not every day I let someone run a bill as high as yours." What, 8-Arms grins, "did you think I would just let you take my inventory, my money, and not expect anything back in return? What kind of business creature would I be then, huh?" His goons, a pair of Atlantic Wolffish with snaggletooth grins and grungy derby hats, chuckle from the shadows. "Did you think you could outsmart me? I have more intelligence in my pinkie tentacles than you nerdy dolphins do."

"Ha ha ha," one of his goons says, drifting out of the shadows. "Tell 'em, boss."

The dolphin nervously pushes his glasses further up his nose. "It was your goons who stole my shipment and made it impossible for me to sell the inventory and pay you back. Please, give me one more chance."

"Well, this right here just happens to be your last chance," 8-Arms growls. "Now," he passes the dolphin with glasses a coral sheet rock, "if you'd like to swim out of here, sign over the Argonauts to me." The dolphin shakes as he signs the coral sheet rock. Before he can say another word, 8-Arms motions for his bodyguards to escort the dolphin away. As the dolphin is dragged away, his cries of "NOOO" are drowned out by the roaring of the crowd as the two teams take their places on the court. 8-Arms leans in and squints at his new team and then at the scoreboard where the Tridents' name is glistening, so the whole stadium knows they're winning. That won't do at all, 8-Arms thinks to himself.

"Boys," he says to his goons, "we are going to make some changes around here. Firstly, I don't lose. Period. Losers don't sign contracts. Losers don't inspire dozens of mindless fans to buy their products just because their face is on them. Losers!" 8-Arms practically yells, "Don't! Make! Money!" 8-Arms pants and then catches his breath. "Being the top brand of the snack industry was only the beginning. I'm not going to stop at being the most powerful boss in the sea and underworld. Oh no," 8-Arms points to the court and then gestures to the fans in the stadiums. "I'm going to be the most powerful boss in the entire ocean! And," he rubs two tentacles together, making a clink clack sound from his chains and bracelets clinging together. This is his signature sound when 8-Arms is dishing out commands. Lately, it sends shivers down fish spines and spells a great demise for anyone that 8-Arms wants to retire. 8-Arms smacks his iron clamps on the side of the chest "it all starts with taking over the aquaball."

"Yeah, Boss," agrees his two main henchmen. "Of course, boss. You're the best." 8-Arms rolls his eyes at them. "Better than the best?" One of the henchmen suggests.

"The best of the better of the best!" Chimes in the other henchmen. They both nod quickly, and 8-Arms slaps tentacle across his forehead in frustration.

"Why don't you two let me think, and you can do what I pay you for." The two henchmen stop nodding. "Now," continues 8-Arms, "Start scouting for a player on my new team that will bring wins, fear, and intimidation to the other players in the league. A dolphin-like," 8-Arms scans the court and sees Krug sneering at the scoreboard in anger, "Krug," he grins. His two henchmen swim away, and 8-Arms says to himself, "I'm going to own this league, and it starts with this team beating that Odon and anyone who dares to swim in our way. We win the fans; we win the league. We win the league, and my treasure chest will be overflowing with loot."

Suddenly, 8-Arms sees Odon swim the

section of the court in front of his box. 8-Arms jet propels towards Odon to intercept him. Without warning, 8-Arms wraps his tentacle around Odon. Startled, Odon gives him a look that clearly says: say what you want, but don't touch.

"You know I like your swagger, kid, but this league is about to change for the better now that I'm the owner of the Argonauts."

"Wait, How? Why? Hold on. What happened?" asks Odon. "One thing's for sure, Mr. 8-Arms," challenges Odon, "I represent the spirit of teamwork. There is a spirit of fun and appreciation for our skills, talents, and differences in the league. I will do my very best to keep that spirit alive and kicking. I know all about you and what you stand for. I know you care more about

money than anything else, and I won't let that kind of attitude take root in this beautiful game!" Odon shakes loose of 8-Arms' grip and, with a flick of his tail, swims away. Furious, 8-Arms balls each of his tentacles into a tight fist.

"Sir," Krug says from behind 8-Arms, "two, uh, fish said you wanted to see me."

8-Arms spins towards Krug and lets all his anger at Odon out on him. He sticks a tentacle in Krug's face and snaps, "Listen and listen well. I don't tolerate losers, and right now, all I see swimming in front of me is a LOSER. Either you start stepping up, or I'm gonna sit you on the bench, PERMANENTLY. So, do whatever it takes to win, or I'll find someone who can. There's no way that the half-time score needs to stay at 2-1 in favor of the Tridents. You better do better than that in the coming second half, alright? Do we understand each other?" Krug's face pales, and he nods his head. When 8-Arms swims back to the owner's box, Krug looks at the Tridents. Rooks catches his eye, and Krug snarls at him.

"Fish bait!" Krug yells before dashing back to his team. Rooks shakes with anticipation.

"Odon," Solitaire asks as he swims next to

Rooks to comfort him. "Was that who I think it was talking to Krug?"

"Yea," Odon sighs. "Mr. 8-Arms is now the owner of the Argonauts." Gasps of shock and murmurs of confusion shutter through the team. They all seem a bit worried now that the underworld boss is a part of the league now. Odon, not one to be easily discouraged, sees the dismay on his team's faces and gives them a pep talk before taking the field for the second half of the Ocean Bowl championship game.

"There comes a moment when you have to believe and have faith in your teammates, skills, and your gifts," Odon reminds them, "and the ones around you who make you strong when you are feeling weak. We will not be intimidated! We

Even though it has the word whale in its name, the short-finned pilot whale is not actually a whale. They're a dolphin! Just like their cold-water cousins, these dolphins live in close family pods for their entire lives. That's right, when baby short-finned pilot whales are born into a pod, they get to grow up within the safety of that pod, too. Nicknamed the "cheetah of the deep sea", this ultra-fast dolphin is known for its high speeds and deep dives to catch its favorite food. In fact, they eat about 70lbs of octopus and squid a day. But don't worry, Squiddy is safe from the short-finned pilot whale because these dolphins prefer deep, warm waters to live in. If you wanted to find one, they can be found in the Caribbean, near Mexico, and North Africa, as well as other places around the world.

"Short-Finned Pilot Whale." Whale & Dolphin Conservation USA, January 24, 2020.

https://us.whales.org/whales-dolphins/species-guide/short-finned-pilot-whale/

will not give in to the fear they want us to feel so

that we won't play our best. This is that moment, squad. As my good friend, Jay, used to say to me, 'I got 99 problems, but this isn't one of them.' So today, my friends, my Tridents, today is not one of our 99 problems. Krug and Mr. 8-Arms aren't one of our problems. Today, it's 'we' instead of 'me.' And as a team, we got this! Let's go get it!"

As Odon finishes getting his teammates pumped up and ready to fight in the second half, the announcer, a short-finned pilot whale, tries to distract the restless crowd with a little entertainment, "Some say he has made and sold over 5 billion fish cakes for the sea world! Some say he doesn't sleep because of the hundred jobs he has. Some say, don't make the big shy guy mad, or he will turn into the incredible red hulk of squids. He is the best chef, team doctor,

and bandleader in the entire sea world! The man.

The myth. The legend. Give it up for Squiddy!"

Squiddy smoothly glides over and takes

to the lagoon stage. In his six tentacles, he has an old bass drum, a top half of a shell that he uses as a cymbal, a snare, a discarded old horn, a microphone shell, and a beat-up violin, which he uses to play a rhythm with a beatbox type of vibe: **Boom-boom-click! Boom-boom-click!**

Squiddy instructs the crowd, "Okay, Okay. Put your fins, flippers, and wings together. And it goes like this: Work hard! Boom-boom-click! "Play hard!" Boom-boom. Boom-boom-click "Score hard!" Boom-boom-click. "Go hard." Boom-boom. "Go hard!"

Once the crowd repeats the hook with the bass beat, Squiddy raps the entire replay:

Odon takes the ball and speeds around the court.

He busts through the lines like he's kicking down the door,
Krug's making moves,
Tridents in shame, Get ready y'all,

IT'S ANY TEAM'S GAME!

As Squiddy starts to go hard on the drums, the audience roars with excitement and is full of Ocean Bowl fan energy. Squiddy decides to get the hype higher and 'turn up.' Squiddy steps away from the drums and starts swaying. Left, right, left: the crowd is standing on their feet as Squiddy starts doing a three-step and then a four-step count dance move. They start to chant, "Do the 'Squiddy rock'! Do the 'Squiddy rock'! Do the 'Squiddy rock.'" Squiddy is more than appeasing and gets more into his dance moves. The crowd loves it and joins in with their rendition.

Meanwhile, as the excitement builds, all over the Ocean-net, and on the seaweed social media networks, news of the play-by-play and pics are blowing up. Just over on the other side of the lagoon are some other dolphins jumping and having a blast waiting for the game to pick back up in the second half. Overhead, the seagulls and other birds share the news about the game with the rest of the sea world that can't be in attendance via shell phones and the Shell News Station.

Halftime is now over, and it's back to the action between the Argonauts and the Tridents. As both teams prepare to take the Ocean Bowl lagoon courts, Krug remembers what 8-Arms said to him and uses it as fearful motivation for himself. Krug muscles his way straight out the gate and steals the passing ball from Rooks and "takes it to the house" to shoot the ball into the giant clam goal, scoring one point, and pushing his team to a tie with the Tridents, 2 to 2. A muscle in Krug's jaw tightens as he thinks, I'm unstoppable! He zigs zags around the court and flies past Odon and Solitaire. Now Krug can feel and see that the Tridents are tired by the way they're dragging their flippers.

Krug swims a tight circle around Odon. "What's wrong little minnow? Can't keep up with the real dolphins?" Then Krug jets back to his team, leaving Odon in a trail of his bubbles.

Odon grits his teeth. "I can do this," he whispers to himself. When the referee blows the whistle, Odon keeps his eyes on Krug. Every move Krug makes, Odon is his shadow. Krug looks behind him and sees Odon mimic his every move.

Krug sneers, "Catch me if you can!" Then, fast as a whip, he lunges down the court with the ball. At first, Odon is right behind him, but soon, he starts to fall behind. Odon must surface more than often now to take big gulping breaths through his dolphin blowhole as Krug pulls further and further ahead, driving straight for the goal again. Krug does a complete stop, with Rooks a few yards in front of him, just within the 1-meter marker, and jumps from the water into the air with the aquaball in his mouth. He shoots the ball over Rooks to school another goal. "Oh boy! Krug is on fire now. The score is now 3 to 2, Argonauts," says the announcer.

A sharp blast of a whistle signals to both teams that Odon has called a timeout. Krug does a victory lap to show the Tridents just how much more energy he has than they do. He doesn't need a timeout. Odon tries not to glare at Krug's showboating as he chugs a 'dolphinator-aid' sports drink.

"Everything okay?" Bon asks Odon.

Odon bends over and tries his best to catch his breath. He didn't think trying to keep up with Krug would wear him down this much. He says to himself. I'm giving it everything I've got, and we're still barely hanging in there. I don't know how much more I've got left in the tank. "I'm just a little," Odon looks at Krug, who's flexing his tail muscle for the cameras. "Distracted, I guess."

Odon sighs and looks down. "I used my Speed Blast a few times too many in the first half, so now I guess it's catching up to me and making me feel a little tired."

"I feel ya. But remember, you don't HAVE to beat anyone. We're here because we want to have a good time. We're the best because we work hard for it. And when we work hard at something we love, everything else will fall into place."

Odon smiles and feels some of the pressure he's put on himself fade away. "You, know what, you're pretty wise, Bon."

"You mean the wisest!" he laughs. "Somebody else wise just told me that we might have 99 problems, but Krug isn't one."

"True that!" Odon says. He feels re-energized and ready to put his best fin forward now. "Let's go; we got this!" Odon leads his teammates back to the playing field. They dip their heads in and out of the water and then slap fins. They jump and rocket straight up and then back into the water—they complete the post timeout ritual by blowing water from their blowholes.

"Let's go, fellas!" cheers Solitaire. Their show of team spirit sparks cheers and reassures their fans they haven't given up and are pumped up to win the championship.

Meanwhile, on the other side of the court, Krug and Brig are debating the best tactics to win the game. Even though Brigs comes up with several different plays that he thinks would be great, Krug dismisses them all.

"They're not good enough," he hisses.

"You don't know that. We have to try--"

"--Trying isn't good enough!" Krug slams the playbook out of Brigs' fins. He envisions 8-Arms threats flashing in his head like hundreds of overlapping paparazzi camera flashes. LOSER. BENCH. PERMANENTLY. Krug shakes his head to try and clear the haze from his thoughts. The buzzer rings out that the time out is over, and mincingly Krug says, "I got this." He swims over to one of his teammates and whispers quietly in his ear as he gestures toward Bon.

When they get back to the court, one of

the Argonauts recklessly swims straight at Bon and turns hard right so that he slaps Bon's melon area on his head with his tail. Bon sees stars dancing above his head. The referee penalizes the Argonauts one point and signals for the Tridents to resume play. Rooks convinces Solitaire and Odon to pass the ball between themselves and play keep away until Bon has a chance to recover. Because of the penalty to the Argonauts, the score is now tied again at 2 to 2.

After a missed shot by the Tridents' Bon, Briggs rebounds and passes the ball to another player on the Argonauts, who drives it past Solitaire, narrowly squeezing by Rooks and scoring one point and puts his team up again.

"THREE-TWO," says the announcer. "It's

still close, y'all, and it's anybody's game, now!"

Looking at the scoreboard and the countdown clock, Odon knows exactly what he needs to do. He turns to his team and subtly says, "I need the Okie Dokie to play."

Unfortunately, Solitaire is the only one to notice the call from Odon. As Odon passes the ball to Rooks, Krug dashes in and seizes the opportunity to steal the ball and jets with the aquaball on his head towards the Trident giant clam goal. He pulls up for a two-pointer jumper, and he scores again! Argonauts lead 5 to 2 on the Tridents. Krug looks up to the owner's box. 8-Arms gives Krug an assured look of confidence.

Krug smirks and uses his tail to push a wave towards Odon., "Yes, in your face!" he says.

Odon shakes his head and swims away without a word. Seeing that his friend's spirits are going down again, Rooks rallies the crowd until they are cheering, "Let's go, Tridents, let's go!"

"They should be cheering for the winners!" Krug growls. "Winners are all anyone should care about. Nobody would like a loser, because if they did, it wouldn't matter if we won or lost, and Mr. 8-Arms wouldn't threaten to bench me." Frustrated with the attention Rooks gets, Krug completely ignores the rules for sports-fish-ship conduct and steamrolls Rooks right into the crowd. Krug looks up to the 8-Arms owners' box to get some assurance and approval of the devious move.

With shock and awe, "What in the world

did you just do? You just cost me the game," 8-Arms screams from the owner's area. Before he knows what hit him, the referee tosses Krug from the game and penalizes the Argonauts one point again! A disappointing 'emote' graphic appears on the Ocean Bowl game screen.

Odon and the team look at each other to signify that this is their time to come back and win. With Krug gone and the score now 4 to 2 in favor of the Argonauts, Odon and his Tridents have a much easier time handling the Argonauts. Bon passes the ball to Odon, who spins it towards Rooks. Then Rooks flips it towards Solitaire, goes 'hype-mode,' and torpedoes it towards the goal. DING! One more point for the Tridents making the score Argonauts 4 - Tridents 3. Next, Odon pulls out one more speed play and slams the ball into the goal. DING! DING! Tridents tie the game 4 to 4!

As the game clock counts down to the final minute, Bon tosses an 'alley-oop' ball to Odon. Odon misses the dunk into the giant clam goal. Solitaire rebounds and passes it back to a recovered Odon who can see a clear shot, but he headbutts the ball to Rooks with thirty seconds left on the clock. Faking left and then bobbing right, Rooks drives the ball straight to the left side of the goal. He stands tall in the wavy, turquoise waters on his back fluke and shoots the aquaball off the backboard of the giant clam. "GOOOOOAAAAAL!" the announcer shouts. Rooks scores one last point for the Tridents. Fish chips from the bags being held by the Ocean Bowl crowd are flying everywhere as the crowd is amazed and shocked by the game outcome. Plankton and tropical flowers explode from behind the scoreboard as the announcer practically screams, "The Tridents comeback with a victorious final score of 5 to 4 over the Argonauts!" This has 8-Arms twirling his tentacles around and around. Then in his anger, he turns red with envy and storms out with his treasure chest in tow. "Someday, man. Someday soon, Odon, I will win and win it all," says 8-Arms in a sly, devious tone. "I won't be denied."

Anna appears with Scooter, the green turtle, to help present the most valuable player trophy and a team trophy.

"Congratulations, Tridents!" says Anna.

Odon gracefully accepts the MVP award

with a great big smile, and Bon snags the first aquaball clamshell trophy of the aquaball league championships.

"Ocean Bowl 1 champions, baby," shouts Bon. He shares the trophy with the rest of the team, Rooks and Solitaire.

Meanwhile, the celebration has started. Squiddy is doing the 'Squiddy rock' as the biggest marching band, and The Boom Boom Box is laying down some sick beats. Led by their drumline leader, a beluga whale, is moving and grooving as he beatboxes into a microphone at the head of the band. The band has their trumpets blare as they play a victory march for the Tridents. Fans everywhere start to swarm as they chant, "Tridents! Tridents! Tridents!" Odon comes to the Ocean Bowl courts center on a podium with flowers and water splashing from fans. Krug throws his sponge towel down and turns to storm off, thinking about how his life and career are over from this one loss. Odon leans into the mic and says, "Give it up to the Argonauts!" Krug pauses, stunned. "They were tough," Odon continues. He nods in acknowledgment at Krug, who gives him a half-smile before leaving.

"This won't be the last you see of me, Odon. I'll keep bringing it every time," Krug says to himself. Behind him, he can hear Odon say into the mic, "I was getting a little tired, but my team and I pulled it out." From the podium, Odon points to his teammates, "I'm proud of you, boys! Ocean Bowl 1 is only the beginning y'all. Let's Get it!!!"

The Ocean Bowl 1 became the match that lit the fiery rivalry between the Argonauts and the Tridents. Now, the Ocean Bowl championship series is the most-watched and exciting sport played by the dolphins.

A NEW BEGINNING

Twelve sun and moons have passed since that Ocean Bowl championship game. Odon, with his most goofy and joyous smile, is very excited. He and Anna are having twins.

A golden-brown female dolphin calf jets and jumps on Odon. Then, she is joined in their father's jumping by a pushy male calf that looks a little like Odon with his dark blue body with white stripes that resemble wavy lightning bolts.

Anna joins in on the fun and games. "Let's call our boy Azzacca, which means the spirit of the sea," suggests Anna.

"Zac for short. I love it," says Odon. "And how about Oria for our girl?" Odon suggests. "This is for her golden glow, energy, and joyous attitude. She's pretty like you Anna. She is an

Orcaella snubfin dolphin with golden brownish skin tone."

"You know what? That matches her," says Anna.

Odon makes a promise to his newborn twins, "I'm going to be the best dad ever and, if you want to, I'm going to see about making you two aquaball stars." The twins roll around each other and make Anna and Odon laugh. "Boy, these two are full of energy. Little ones, there's still someone you haven't met yet. Let's go see Jay," says Odon.

Jay is chilling after practicing on his boat with his GTC. He aims and shoots out his grappling hook. Then he turns the dial to the label that says, 'Water Jet Pack.' "I can't wait to test you out more safely. I think it best to hold on to this for now," Jay laughs as he remembers what happened in his first tests.

Odon, Anna, and Oria each pop their heads out of the water on Jay's boat's starboard side. "Hey, buddy! I heard I had company. Where's the other..." Just as Jay is about to finish his question, Zac jumps out and splashes him. With a WTH (what the heck) emote look on his face, Jay just holds his hands out and mouth open with disgust

Did You Know? No.11

Bottlenose dolphins are pregnant for 12 months! When calves are born, they stay with their mother as she teaches them how to breathe, swim and play with their food! One group of dolphins off the coast of Australia have taught their young to use tools such as sponges to protect their snouts when scouting for food on the ocean floor. Since bottlenose dolphins have such a long gestation time or time that mothers have to be pregnant with their babies, twins are rare in dolphins, making Zac and Oria very special.

Lee, Kevin. "The Life Cycle of Bottlenose Dolphins," March 2, 2019.

https://sciencing.com/life-cycle-bottlenose-dolphins-8698262.html

as he was just surprised by Zac.

Odon signals for Jay to use his GTC to translate so they can communicate. Jay throws on his headphones.

"Jay, meet the newest team members to our pod squad.: Oria, and the one that got you all wet up is Azzacca. We call him Zac for short," says Odon. Zac splashes Jay again as if to say, "you better not forget about me!" Jay shrugs but smiles. "Alright, little amigo, it's on!" Jay throws off his sandals and gets ready to jump into the warm, clear waters in JamRock Bay.

They all try to catch Zac, but he's pretty quick. Odon looks at Anna, "I better give them some help to catch Zac. It looks like he has that new speed." Anna smiles.

"Let's go. I got this, guys," says Odon.

"No way, team. We got this," says Jay and Anna as they chase after Zac.

Zac laughs, giggles, and belches as he Zoom Zoom's passed Oria.

If you ever see dolphins in a super-pod migrating, they could likely be heading to partake in cheering the most beautiful game in the sea and their favorite aquaball team. Go Ocean Bowl!

The End

Did You Know?

Did You Know? No.1

The northern right whale and the southern right whale are two different species of whale? While they're not the same, they do have one thing in common: both of them are missing their dorsal fin! Instead, they have sloping foreheads, slimmer tails, and smaller flukes that make them more streamlined. These evolved, organic body parts allow them to make longer leaps and bounce over the ocean's surface.

"Northern Right Whale Dolphin," January 24, 2020.

https://us.whales.org/whales-dolphins/species-guide/northern-right-whale-dolphin/.

"Southern Right Whale Dolphin," January 24, 2020.

https://us.whales.org/whales-dolphins/species-guide/southern-right-whale-dolphin/

Echolocation is when dolphins produce high-frequency clicks in their nasal passage that passes through the melon, the fatty, rounded region of their forehead, which directs the sounds outwards. These sounds bounce off an object or creature in the ocean and echo back through the fatty cavity in the dolphin's jawbone. These evolved, organic body parts allow dolphins to navigate, communicate, or detect objects on or under the water's surface. Dolphins aren't the only animals to use echolocation, either. Owing to their poor eyesight and aided by their large ears, bats also use echolocation to navigate and find food.
"How Do Dolphins Communicate?" October 21, 2020.

https://us.whales.org/whales-dolphins/how-do-dolphins-communicate/

Did You Know? No.3

Dolphins must stay awake to breathe! So, if they can't breathe when they are asleep, when do they sleep? Dolphins sleep by only using one half of their brain at a time. Isn't that wild!

"How Do Dolphins Sleep?" Whale & Dolphin Conservation USA, April 16, 2020.

http://www.biologicaldiversity.org/campaigns/fisheries/index.html

Did You Know? No.4

Dolphins must stay awake to breathe! So, if they can't breathe when they are asleep, when do they sleep? Dolphins sleep by only using one half of their brain at a time. Isn't that wild!

"How Do Dolphins Sleep?" Whale & Dolphin Conservation USA, April 16, 2020.

https://us.whales.org/whales-dolphins/how-do-dolphins-sleep/

Dolphins can sense changes and dangers in their environment, like an oncoming tropical storm or a hurricane. Scientists think this response might be because they detect a saltwater difference after a large number of freshwater rainfalls. With their strong survival instinct and intelligence, they can take precautions to stay safe, dive deep, or swim out into deeper waters. Dunn, Jon. "What Do Dolphins Do during Storms?" August 19, 2020.

https://www.discoverwildlife.com/animal-facts/mammals/what-do-dolphins-do-during-storms/

There are many stories of dolphins saving people and other animals, including other dolphins! It is common for dolphins to help the sickly pod mates by swimming alongside them to reach the surface and breathe in the wild. While there are many different ideas of why dolphins help people, one theory is that dolphins can use their echolocation to hear a human's heartbeat and then sense that the person is in danger.

Dolphins-World. "Dolphins Rescuing Humans." Accessed February 10, 2021.

https://www.dolphins-world.com/dolphins-rescuing-humans/

Did You Know? No.7

In the great blue ocean, many types of dolphins hang in groups called "pods." They can range in size from anywhere from 2-30 members. However, they can also form "superpods" in deeper parts of the ocean containing thousands of dolphins. Another type of dolphin pod is a juvenile pod. Juvenile pods include both males and females, but males often stay in these pods longer. Dolphins use whistles to communicate with each other. Every dolphin has a unique whistle pattern, called a "signature whistle."

"Dolphin Facts and Information." Whale & Dolphin Conservation USA, November 30, 2020.

https://us.whales.org/whales-dolphins/facts-about-dolphins/#:~:text=The%20smallest%20dolphins&text=A%20group%20of%20dolphins%20is,for%20food%20as%20a%20team

Dolphins love to play! In fact, playing is not all fun and games for them. When dolphins play, they are also learning about social cues, creating strong bonds, and entertaining their highly intelligent minds. Dolphin's sleek bodies can perform acrobatic leaps and spins above the surface of the water, and they can even be observed in something that looks like play fighting with each other and forming strong bonds. We often see wild dolphins playing with a field of seagrass and other objects in their environment like snail egg casings. However, even though dolphins are playful and friendly by nature, like wild animals, it is important not to force ourselves into their space and observe them from afar. It is best to let dolphins be dolphins! We can view them in the wild safely, free of human interaction.

Kuczaj, S. A., & Eskelinen, H. C. (2014). Why do dolphins play? Animal Behavior and Cognition, 1(2), 113-127. doi: 10.12966/abc.05.03.2014

Did You Know? No.9

The octopus is considered by most scientists to be the most intelligent of all the invertebrates (animals without a backbone) and may be as smart as a Golden Retriever dog. This fact is because each of its eight arms has its own 'mini-brain,' connected to the main brain in its head by a network of neurons, of which it has around 500 million! Each arm can move independently and make quick decisions, making them masters of escaping. They can show complex problem-solving skills such as the ability to free themselves from the inside of a closed jar or often find unique ways to escape from aquarium habitats. In the undersea environment, the octopus can outwit predators by changing color for camouflage or releasing a thick black cloud of ink into the water to mask their retreat. If one arm is lost or damaged in an accident, in time, it can grow back!

Newman, Alan. "Alan Newman," October 5, 2016.

http://www.scijourner.org/2016/05/20/the-magic-of-arm-regrowth/#:~:text=Octopi%20regenerate%20lost%20arms%20just,grow%20into%20a%20new%20octopus.&text=As%20soon%20as%20the%20arm,immediately%20begins%20its%20

regeneration%20process

"Octopuses Keep Surprising US - Here Are Eight Examples How." Accessed February 11, 2021.

https://www.nhm.ac.uk/discover/octopuses-keep-surprising-us-here-are-eight-examples-how.html#:~:text=Octopuses%20have%20about%20as%20many

Did You Know? No.10

Even though it has the word whale in its name, the short-finned pilot whale is not actually a whale. They're a dolphin! Just like their cold-water cousins, these dolphins live in close family pods for their entire lives. That's right, when baby short-finned pilot whales are born into a pod, they get to grow up within the safety of that pod, too. Nicknamed the "cheetah of the deep sea," this ultra-fast dolphin is known for its high speeds and deep dives to catch its favorite food. In fact, they eat about 70lbs of octopus and squid a day. But don't worry, Squiddy is safe from the short-finned pilot whale because these dolphins prefer deep, warm waters to live in. If you wanted to find one, they can be found in the Caribbean, near Mexico, and North Africa, as well as other places around the world.

"Short-Finned Pilot Whale." Whale & Dolphin Conservation USA, January 24, 2020.

https://us.whales.org/whales-dolphins/species-guide/short-finned-pilot-whale/

Bottlenose dolphins are pregnant for 12 months! When calves are born, they stay with their mother as she teaches them how to breathe, swim and play with their food! One group of dolphins off the coast of Australia have taught their young to use tools such as sponges to protect their snouts when scouting for food on the ocean floor. Since bottlenose dolphins have such a long gestation time or time that mothers have to be pregnant with their babies, twins are rare in dolphins, making Zac and Oria very special.

Lee, Kevin. "The Life Cycle of Bottlenose Dolphins," March 2, 2019.

https://sciencing.com/life-cycle-bottlenose-dolphins-8698262.html

"Sponge-Wielding Bottlenose Dolphin," May 18, 2018.

https://ocean.si.edu/ocean-life/marine-mammals/sponge-wielding-bottlenose-dolphin#:~:text=carries%20a%20sponge%2C%20which%20it,daughters%2C%20but%20not%20their%20sons

SCOOTER HERE AGAIN, LETS PLAY SOME OCEAN BOWL GAMES.

137

Ocean Bowl 'Edutainment'

ACTIVITIES

YEA !!! ALLOWANCE

Zac and Oria must collect the hundredths of clam coins allowance given to them from their father Odon.

Name the hundredths digit in each number belov

456	The answer is: 4	91205	
983		21974	
5682		1912	
4560		6511	
478		111	

Word Search

```
V E S A U S L L A A A E I T Z A O F
K D T T Q A O R S R K N T M A R G Q
Y U T R E U L R Z O T G E D C G F V
S T Q O I A A S I M M I C O U O R I
S A H B Y D M B K A A N H L C N I I
Q I S D N L E L A R T E N P I A B N
U N I T X Y J N R L H E O H S U Y U
I M G C H F X M T I L R L I T T R O
D E L T J I X L H S F I O N E S L D
D N O C E A N B O W L N G S M H X O
Y T R V E T Y Z U H E G Y X G F H N
T V S C I E N C E Y W Y Y U H B P W
```

Find the following words in the puzzle.
Words are hidden → ↓ and ↘ .

AQUABALL	MATH	STEM
ARGONAUTS	OCEANBOWL	TECHNOLOGY
ART	ODON	TRIDENTS
DOLPHINS	ORIA	ZAC
EDUTAINMENT	SCIENCE	
ENGINEERING	SQUIDDY	
JAY	STEAM	

DRAW A PICTURE OF YOURSELF HERE. IMAGINE WHAT YOUR AVATAR OR CHARACTER WOULD BE IN THE OCEAN BOWL.

Whatzzzz Up?! I'm ______________________________

and I am a change agent.

AQUABALL DIVISIONS (Page 1)

Draw an arrow to the areas where you have been (on vacation, visited, lived).

Colors: Blue (Artic), Green (Caribbean), Red (Pacific), Yellow (Atlantic)

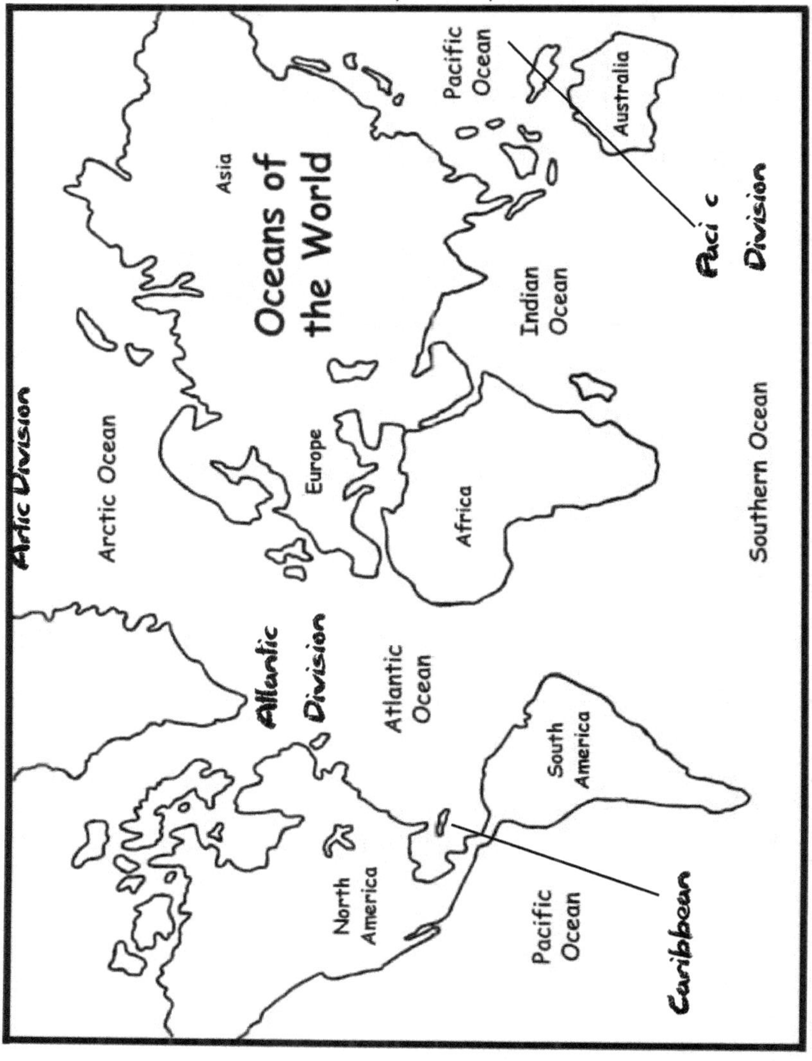

Oceans of the World

Artic Division

Arctic Ocean

Asia

Pacific Ocean

Australia

Paci c Division

Indian Ocean

Europe

Africa

Southern Ocean

Atlantic Division

Atlantic Ocean

North America

South America

Pacific Ocean

Caribbean

AQUABALL DIVISIONS (Page 2)

Here are some aquallball teams names: Tridents,

Cyclones, Argonauts, Harpoons, Torpedos,

____________________, __________________

What division are the Tridents playing in? Have you ever

been to this part of our planet?

____

____

____

Tell us what division would you visit?

____

____

____

Can you list the dolphins that exist in the Artic Ocean?

What about Pacific and Southern Ocean?

____

____

AQUABALL
THE BEAUTIFUL GAME IN THE SEA

Help Boots Score. Get through the maze.

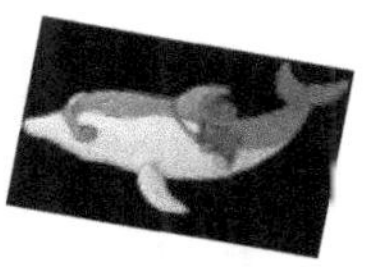

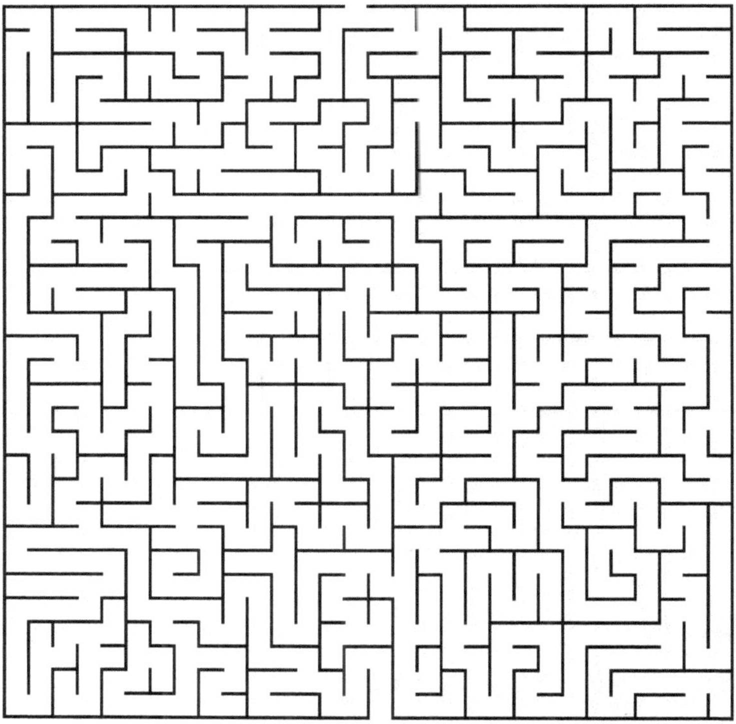

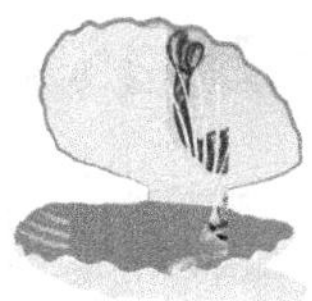

CROSSWORD PUZZLE

DOWN

1. WHAT KIND OF DOLPHIN IS TOO SHORT TWO?
3. WHAT KIND OF MINERAL IS IN THE OCEAN'S WATER?
5. _________ HELPS PROTECT MARINE WILDLIFE.
7. HE IS ALWAYS HUNGRY AND AN ATLANTIC HUMPBACK DOLPHIN.

ACROSS

2. _________ RESULT FROM THE GRAVITATIONAL ATTRACTION OF
THE SUN AND MOON ON THE OCEANS OF THE EARTH.
4. HE OWNS A SUCCESSFUL PLANKTON FISH CHIP BUSINESS
AND BECAME THE SOLE OWNER OF THE ARGONAUTS.
6. WHAT IS ANOTHER TERM FOR OCEAN?
8. HER NAME MEANS "means "wind, sunrise or golden haired".

JAY IS IN HIS LAB

Jay is working on his GTC. He is trying to figure out how many more gadgets can he add to his device. He has to do some math to make sure all his cool ideas fit within the gadget capsules.

He has eight tools already. Jay believes he can fit up two times that amount.

Multiply: 8 × 2=

Jay loses count of the new baby dolphins (calves). There are 42 new ones. **What number multiplied by 7 equals 42**?

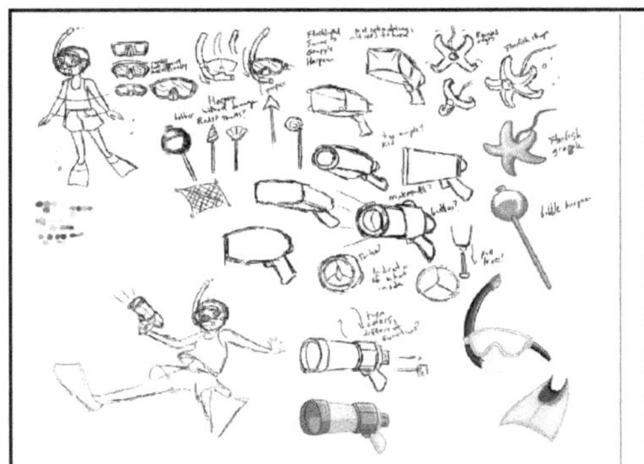

Jay has to divide his fish catch with some local friends in his hometown of JamRock Bay. He is looking to divide 5 fish between 8 persons.

8 × 5 = 40

_____ ÷ 5 = 8

Jay has 324 pounds of trash and debris from his walk-through in JamRock Bay with his grappling hook. Question:
Select all the expressions that are equal to 324.
Answer Options:
A. 372 - 48
B. 660 - 346
C. 119 + 215
D. 728 - 404
E. 216 + 108

SAVE JAY FROM THE RIPTIDES

FILL THE BLANKS FOR YOUR DAY AT THE OCEAN BOWL BEACH

Hey you! My name is _______________ and let me tell you
(YOUR NAME)

about my crazy day at the beach with my Ocean Bowl

friends. On an incredibly hot day, _______________,
(YOU)

_______________, Jay and his Uncle whom he called
(A FRIENDS' NAME)

_______________________________ decided to
(HOW DO YOU SAY UNCLE IN SPANISH?)

anchor the boat and head to the beach.

_______________ packed a bag full of _____________
(FRIEND)   (ADJECTIVE)

___________ and a big jug of __________.
(FOOD)   (LIQUID)

_______________ brought a towel that had a picture of
(A FRIENDS' NAME)

Pinky, the _______________ sea star on it.
(FAVORITE COLOR)

The beach was crowded but there were a few

___________ spots left.
(ADJECTIVE)

___________ and _________ wanted to learn how to
(YOU)   (FRIEND)

___________ so they rented a pair of ______________
(VERB)   (PLURAL NOUN)

and hopped into the water to swim with __________.
                                                 (ODON'S SON)

Soon it was time for more snacks so _____________ went to
                                             (FRIEND)

a stand to buy crab cakes snacks and ______________ while
                                             (PLURAL FOOD)

Tio ________ some fish he caught earlier.
     (VERB)

A lifeguard blew ____________on his ___________ because
                      (TOOL)   (BODY PART)

someone was _____________ too far into the ocean. The sun
                 (-ING VERB)

was _____________ so ____________ and ___________
      (-ING VERB)   (ODON'S SON)   (FRIEND)

rubbed _____________ on each other for protection. The
(NOUN)

lifeguard started to notice what looked to be the start of

rip tides (also known as rip currents).* Eventually the rip

current came too close so we retreated back to the beach.

_____________________ had an awesome day at the beach!
(PLURAL PRONOUN)

_____________ and _____________ packed their _________ and
(FRIEND)   (FRIEND)   (NOUN)

went home.

*Read Book 2 of the Ocean Bowl series titled **Orias' Rippn'
Adventure** to learn more about rip currents also known as rip
tides.

To find more cool edutainment, 1) go to our website Ocean-
bowlbook.com 2) Register your certificate with the date that
you read the book and 3) and receive access to the games and
activities.

Congrats! Date Completed:

____

**Let your teacher or parent know and the
Ocean Bowl team will send some goodies
to your school.**

This awesome sauce

Certification of Achievement

goes to

(Your name)________________________

Keep reading books!
Remember to Reuse or Recycle

ANSWER KEYS

SOLUTION

Word Search

```
.  E  S  A  .  .  .  A  .  E  .  Z  A  .  .
.  D  T  T  Q  .  O  .  R  .  N  T  .  A  R  .  .
.  U  .  R  E  U  .  R  .  .  T  G  E  D  C  G  .  .
.  T  .  .  I  A  A  .  I  .  M  I  C  O  .  O  .  .
S  A  .  .  .  D  M  B  .  A  A  N  H  L  .  N  .  .
Q  I  .  .  .  .  E  .  A  .  T  E  N  P  .  A  .  .
U  N  .  .  .  .  .  N  .  L  H  E  O  H  S  U  .  .
I  M  .  .  .  .  .  .  T  .  L  R  L  I  T  T  .  O
D  E  .  .  J  .  .  .  .  S  .  I  O  N  E  S  .  D
D  N  O  C  E  A  N  B  O  W  L  N  G  S  M  .  .  O
Y  T  .  .  .  .  Y  .  .  .  G  Y  .  .  .  .  N
.  .  S  C  I  E  N  C  E  .  .  .  .  .  .  .  .  .
```

Word directions and start points are formatted: (Direction, X, Y)

AQUABALL (SE,4,1)	MATH (S,11,4)	STEM (S,15,7)
ARGONAUTS (S,16,1)	OCEANBOWL (E,3,10)	TECHNOLOGY (S,13,2)
ART (SE,9,1)	ODON (S,18,8)	TRIDENTS (SE,3,2)
DOLPHINS (S,14,3)	ORIA (SE,7,2)	ZAC (S,15,1)
EDUTAINMENT (S,2,1)	SCIENCE (E,3,12)	
ENGINEERING (S,12,1)	SQUIDDY (S,1,5)	
JAY (SE,5,9)	STEAM (SE,3,1)	

ABOUT THE CREATOR AND AUTHOR

Roman Sudan Montagueo is the creator and author of the Ocean Bowl "edutainment" series. Edutainment (educational entertainment) is an engaging way to get kids of all colors to enjoy an entertaining story while learning facts in the fields of science, technology, engineering, art, and math. He is the father two awesome children. He holds advanced degrees and advanced studies in Organizational Leadership, Information Technology, Business Psychology, and Product Development.

**Educational entertainment to meet the mission:
Literacy + S.T.E.A.M. + Conservation**

http://oceanbowlseries.com/
Twitter,YouTube and Instagram:
@OceanBowlSeries   @domsudan2

OTHER TITLES
Catch up with you in the next book:

ORIAS RIPPIN ADVENTURE

AND

ZAC AND ORIA
MAKE A SPLASH

FREE GIFTS/EMAIL LIST

FOLLOW US AND SUBSCRIBE ON YOUTUBE AND TWITCH.

JOIN THE EMAIL LIST:
OCEANBOWL9@GMAIL.COM

DEDICATION

"Hi Mom!" "This book series is dedicated to my two kids, family, and friends."

ACKNOWLEDGMENT

Format and Layout - A'lysia Alcorn
Proofing and Project Assistant - Sierra Sigmone
Public Relations Assistant - Isha Kamara
Contributors - George Nunez and Akilah Stevens

WHO HELPED TO MAKE THIS BOOK BETTER IN 2021?

"The editor Victoria Weber was there to watch our backs and make sure we didn't release a second edition with spelling and grammar mistakes all over the place."

Bio-
I loves to read and always have! I am an elementary school teacher and have a Master's Degree in Teaching and Learning. I have an endorsement in ESL which means that my job is to facilitate English language acquisition to students who speak a language other than English. As such, I have constant experience with editing and revision. I have also worked with self-published authors on children's books and novels of varying lengths and genres. - Victoria Weber, MSc from Miliken University

"The marine biologist Jasmine Rose was there to share her love for the mission and vision of this book series by reading the book and writing a foreword for it."

Bio-
I was born in England, but was raised across the world. I was lucky enough to grow up in some of the most beautiful parts, mainly across Asia. spent many of childhood years at the Red Sea, where I saw  the most amazing sights. This is where my love for the ocean started and my passion to preserve our marine world.

I studied Marine Biology both at Falmouth Marine
School, in Cornwall UK and at the University of
Southampton, UK. I continue to dive and teach people
about the natural world around us and aim to inspire
and ignite the same passion for the oceans, as I have, to
the younger generation. - Jasmine Rose, BSc

Email: Jasmine.a.rose@gmail.com

"She completed the scientific review on Book 3- Make A Splash, so we
had to turn to our favorite 'young gun' and wildlife conservation from
the United Kingdom, Carla Broom to help us out again."

Bio-
I studied Biology and Wildlife Conservation at university,
and since then have worked
on many conservation projects.
One of these involved hosting
whale watching tours and
carrying out cetacean surveys,
so I have pretty good dolphin
knowledge!

Linkedin
https://www.linkedin.com/in/carla-broom-537927158/

**A special thanks to the Clearwater Marine Aquarium
for their collaboration and scientific review.**

Many thanks and blessings everyone -

Roman Sudan Montagueo